THE MATURE MANUAL
101 RELATIONSHIP REMINDERS

THE

MATURE

MANual

101:

RELATIONSHIP

REMINDERS

Author: Sabrina, L • Title: The Mature Manual: 101 Relationship Reminders
Edition: First (1st) • ISBN: 978 1 8381214 0 2 • Description: Paperback

Contents

Foreword

by Keith and Amanda McKenzie

For a relationship to be a positive experience for both involved a lot of investment and commitment is required, as the journey can be rocky and shaken by the many unexpected events that impact on it. As we read this book we were reminded of our challenges and our journey to develop and nurture our relationship. It is very impressive that someone so relatively young could have such an insight and understanding of the complexities involved in sustaining a healthy relationship.

This book cleverly identifies the many facets of the journey and how important honesty, openness and knowing yourself are to ensure and develop a successful union. We found it extremely easy to relate to the *'reminders'* outlined within the book; there was a realisation that they had been integral parts of our own marriage.

Having known Lamara for over two decades, in this book she maintains her positive approach to life and its challenges. She makes it clear that relationships are rarely plain sailing and both parties must put in the hard work if it is to succeed, by concisely identifying challenges and strategies. Lamara is clear in describing and recognising signs that a relationship may be failing or unhealthy and when to call time to avoid hurt and harmful consequences to either party.

This book encapsulates the lessons which I believe Lamara and many young women have learnt. The advice is invaluable to those who are still negotiating the complex and bewildering world of relationships. Above all, Lamara has emphasised the importance for us to take responsibility for our own actions and to have those discussions, as positive relationships do not just happen by accident.

Introduction

The Best Laid Plans

We all have relationships, but we don't always do them well. Imagine a relationship like taking a walk on the beach on a sunny day. The weather is gorgeous and you are feeling the heat from the sun's rays massaging your body. Your temperature rises and you decide to take a walk towards the sea to cool off. The breeze brushes your face as you walk, it smells fresh. You're feeling relaxed and decide to dip your toes into the water. The shallow waters of the sea soothe your feet; you stand still and look out at the landscape feeling content, you exhale. A calm feeling guides you further out into the clear waters. The juxtaposition of the sun kissing your face and the sea soothing your feet is refreshing. You want to savour the feeling. You continue to walk across the seas' shallow waters, you smile to yourself; life is good.

Suddenly, you lose your footing and become submerged under water. You find it hard to catch a breath; you're flailing. You feel the current pulling you further out to sea; your mind is working overtime. The secure sands of the shore are now a memory, how can you get back to safety?

That's the challenge of relationships. Sometimes the perspective of our situation can be so naïve that we take preparation for granted. This is why it is important for me to impart my knowledge and information to the next generation. It is never too late to learn and we can all acquire new ideas to challenge or change our outlook.

See this manual as a reference guide. No, I do not know everything there is to know when it comes to healthy or successful relationships, but I know that what I *do* know is worth sharing. My work as a coach, mentor and experiences both lived and witnessed can offer you something to think about and open up conversations within your own environment.

How have you been in past relationships? Have you learnt

any lessons? How do you fair in current ones, can you swim? Do you need armbands or armour? It takes work to sustain a happy, healthy relationship. Starting with being willing to learn and comprehend a spectrum of behaviours within them, so we can try to avoid the pitfalls.

As women, we are never going to fully understand the ways of men so we cannot afford to assume how we should behave in a relationship. We need to appreciate them for who they are and be honest about the kinds of relationships we want. This will ensure that we are taking decisions based on the information that presents itself, filtered through our evolving knowledge. It is a daily effort, not a blind choice. Are you geared up? Do you have the information or tools necessary for the job?

There are no two relationships that are the same, but every relationship occupies time. Time is the most important commodity we have; this book will encourage you not to waste yours in senseless situations by sharing some tools, tips and tangibles to avoid getting caught up in a spider's web of emotions. These *101 Relationship Reminders* can equally challenge you to assess your own situation and to discern discord early to reduce the pain that comes along with any poor investment. It begins with the relationship you have with yourself first. It is when you have gained this knowledge and sought understanding that you can begin to take a reflective view on how you can apply this information; then use that confidence to act upon it.

Part One

Stand Firm, Stay Positive

As women, we can be as delicate as flowers. Planted as seedlings and absorbing the influences of our environment as we mature. The strength of our stem and leaves determined by how and what we were fed as we grew. When we are exposed to the right circumstances we blossom.

This is similar to women in relationships. We can be very fragile and let men lead us in a direction they choose, which could be astray. We can easily neglect that we were planted before a man ever crossed our path. Many of us began growing and being shaped, or socially conditioned, by our environment without fully grasping the intricacies of relationships and what they entail. Is this why we can allow ourselves to be easily gone with the wind? You've probably heard that people often speak to flowers and plants to help them to grow well, positive words of encouragement are critical. Reflect back on your younger years, who spoke to you as you were growing and being moulded, did you speak to yourself? Analyse what voices influenced your trajectory, were they a help or a hindrance? Did they apply purpose or pressure? Relationships can be lovely, but we should never forget that we are complete people in our own right and need to remain healthy, mind, body and spirit. Not just to grow but to flourish, as it is in this state that we truly excel in relationships.

The reminders in this section have a focus on self to help reassure and affirm that everything starts with you.

Reminders 1 to 18 - *Understanding who you are*

1.   Never try to find a man, find yourself

Who are you, what are your ambitions, what do you like and what do you dislike? Figure this out first, be secure in it. A mature man will find you when you are happily on your own journey!

2.   Be properly rooted

Know who you are and take the time to just be; this will help you sharpen your senses and be firm in who you are until it becomes your default setting.

3.   Rely on self and the energy within

Listen to your intuition and pay attention to how you feel inside. You need to be your own cheerleader first before you can expect anyone else to cheer for you.

4.   Have a strong healthy conviction in who you are

Understand yourself and your values. Is your self-esteem intact? Define who you are for yourself to ensure you stand for something and will not fall for anything.

5.   Work on self

Are there things you have not dealt with, take the time to heal from your past hurts and love yourself so that you can fully heal, mind, body and spirit.

6.   Own your story

What have you been through, are you aware of what has shaped your understanding, are you omitting things that you want to keep hidden? Learn from your past to avoid stunting your growth.

7.   **Know your own journey**

Know the direction you are going in and own your journey. Be mindful not to compare, compete or complain; for your path is your own.

8.   **Don't act the part, 'Be' the part!**

How do you carry yourself; do you own the space in which you are in; are you stepping with grace and confidence. Show gratitude and be your best version of you.

9.   **Take care of self**

If you are not prepared to take good care of you, why should anybody else. Treat yourself well; how do you feel? How do you look? What are you consuming? This teaches others how to treat you.

10.   **Have a vision for your life**

What are your dreams, do you have a focus or is your mind occupied with clutter? Find out where you want to go and begin to take the steps to get there.

11. **Have self-control**

Not everything is for everyone and you do not need to be involved with everybody. Use emotional intelligence to determine how you communicate with others and what is actually worth your time.

12. **Don't accept less**

Respect the power within you and do not give it away by accepting less than you deserve. Set your standards and stick to them. Not everything should be a negotiation.

13. **Self-acceptance**

There is confidence in your individuality, accept yourself by approving and affirming who you are in every facet. Don't waste your time aspiring to be like the rest, trust yourself and work on being the best that you can be using your unique gifts.

14. **Be positive**

You are what you practice. If you practice being positive it will begin to come naturally and will assist you in overcoming challenges, by attracting that same positivity you give.

15. **Take your time**

Work at your own pace and don't be too hard on yourself; take your time as you make progress and remember life is not a race.

16. **Utilise your network**

Are you good with people, what do you bring to the table? Hold on to good like-minded people but don't stifle them; remember to be fair in exchange. What is your offering? Be aware too that people may not be with you for your full journey.

17. **Love yourself**

Actively love yourself by treating yourself well and by speaking positive words into your life. Accept where you are and focus on the actions needed to take you to where you need to be.

18. **Sharpen your 'No'**

Exercise your 'No' regularly; test it out by using it often and standing in that decision with confidence. Keep your 'No' muscle toned and active so that it will be less likely to fail you when you need it most.

Part Two

Giving Ego a Bad Name

So much of the time women give men too much credit for the ideals they conjure up about them. Like any living being, men have their own struggles and a different pressure to manage. The perception of men can precede them. Obtained by stereotype this ideology gets reinforced by the things that they deem to be manly, as represented by social conditioning and accepted by them via ego. This can shut down any ideas to the contrary therefore, women don't always realise a man's insecurities. Given this we can fail to notice when they disguise their fragility behind a façade birthed by their lack of knowledge, money, and respect; so, to them power. Unfortunately, many men see his tenderness as his weakness, but for a man to reach his full potential he needs to accept and relish in the tender influence from the being that first carried him, a woman. Men often do not concede to this and their egos can force them to maintain their hard shell.

Imagine a cocoon with its tough exterior, could you appreciate the sensitivity that lives inside if the ego prevented it from flourishing. Perhaps men don't realise this. Like a caterpillar, an immature or insecure man can be gluttonous and have his fingers in every pie to try and satisfy his appetite; and many do. Such actions may give fleeting satisfaction but creates dis-ease and causes confusion to those involved. These are the types of destructive behaviours, perpetually reflected, that reinforces toxic dynamics in relationships.

Contrast this to a butterfly, gracious in its appearance and so delicate to the touch, they do not go unnoticed. Widely admired and respected, butterflies are observant to camouflage and provide a cover of protection whenever necessary. A calm confidence, an example of its ego is demonstrated in the intricacies of its beautiful wings, this is the influence of a woman. If she is given a safe space to do so, a woman can encourage a caterpillar to break out of his shell and enjoy a power provided by the cover of his wings.

However, he will need to understand his tender strength first and show leadership by example in being prepared and being willing to trust and submit unto her, his woman.

These reminders touch on the qualities you should look out for when accepting a mature man. All men have an ego and rightfully so, but is it misplaced and presenting as insecurity?

Reminders 19 to 34 - *Observations when a Man Presents Himself*

19.   **Be of good character**

> *He lives his life with good integrity and high moral standards which will be reflected in how he consistently behaves.*

20.   **Have ambition**

> *He should be driven, determined and be articulate enough to communicate his plans and vision effectively.*

21.   **Attentiveness**

> *He should be attentive to learn your different needs and requirements and be willing to act upon them.*

22. **Earn your trust**

He should be prepared to work to earn your trust by providing a safe environment for you to express yourself comfortably.

23. **Have more than just potential**

He should be ready and prepared to capitalise on his potential through having a plan and acting upon it.

24. **Be Inspirational**

He should celebrate your ambition and goals and encourage you to be better.

25. **Can express himself**

He should be able to express his feelings to you and see this as strength.

26. **Does not conform to stereotypes**

He does not concede to gimmicks of how men should behave or use those depictions as an excuse for poor choices.

27. **Be held accountable**

He should have ownership in his actions and be willing to explain them as he may not always get things right but welcomes constructive feedback and an opportunity to learn.

28. **Be self-aware**

He should understand his personal shortcomings and the areas where he needs support or improvement and be open to work on these areas.

29. **Vision and goals**

He should have a vision for his life and can outline tangible goals in order to achieve them.

30. **Consider his future family**

He should think about his family or future family that he is working to provide for and the legacy he wants to create.

31. **Have it covered**

He should understand the role he plays in his family or community to safeguard and give cover through provision and protection.

32. Be courageous

He should demonstrate courage by being steadfast in standing up for his beliefs and not be easily led.

33. Leadership skills

He should be aware that a leader does not have to be in the forefront but can effectively direct a team by example and own the outcome whether favourable or not.

34. Does not try to control everything

He should be able to just let things be, especially if it doesn't create hindrance or harm, and see the value in being able to relax.

Part Three

Checkmate

The dating scene can be a complex playground and not all games are played fairly. Often, we don't know the rules of a game, or even how to play. Take Chess, a game of two players where the aim is to 'check' the King. When dating, women can often get too excited or giddy because they take so many things to heart. Some may feel that they are not worthy, and others do too much to make a man feel comfortable without considering their own feelings or comfort levels first. Whether out of insecurities, ignorance or desperation it serves as a distraction and is potentially damaging to take things so personally.

It can be admirable that men want to be a king in our lives, but they should not be given this position lightly; they need to earn it. A king by nature is firm in who he is and what he stands for; he is led by his values and principles. Kings are also accountable for their actions and understand that nothing is without consequence. As with a king, men too need to be held to account, he needs to be corrected or called out where his actions fall out of line. This is vitally important when it comes to inappropriate communication or behaviours, it is not wise to allow things to fester or grow. Raise issues early and work to resolve them to restore balance and prevent toxic outcomes. It could be an accidental occurrence or intentional, either way you are demonstrating the rules of play. This is the practice that displays your self-respect and communicates with men how they can or should treat you, through clarifying what you will or will not tolerate. If rules are repeatedly being broken, then it should be game over! Don't assume that a reprimand is a bitter act; don't accept it as negative or excuse harsh tones and actions to explain it. On the contrary, it can be a display of thoughtful consideration. A true king would welcome this, whether he shows it or not, as it encourages him to become better. If a man will not accept this, decide if he really is on his way to becoming a king or a tyrant.

Ultimately, there's an object to all games, you usually win or lose. Paying attention to the signs that *will* present themselves during the trial or dating phase helps you to see beneath the masks and uncover truths. This will aid you in being sure that the winner has played fairly.

These reminders will give you considerations during the probationary period to discern if your date could become your king. Some people cheat, others may lie so don't rush the play or allow deceitful players to fool you into a *checkmate* position.

Reminders 35 to 78 - *Managing the Data in Dating*

35.   Remember who you are

Do not lose yourself in a relationship. A healthy relationship should bring out the best in you, not bury your blessings.

36.   Are you ready?

Ensure that you are in a healthy space to be dating in the first place. It's ok if you're not ready, don't rush yourself. Don't allow others to push, pressure, force or coerce you to start dating. You are not missing out, take your own time.

37.   **Listen, listen and listen**

Be quiet and pay attention to what he says. Learn more about who he is by asking questions, learn his story; probe further and encourage him to elaborate. Gain an understanding from what he is willing to share.

38.   **Trial period**

What are your terms for this audition or probation period? When will you know the outcome? If there is no response or progress by the time you expect, what will you do? Will you extend the trial period or will you call it a day?

39.   **Walk away**

Are you prepared and willing to walk away if you feel like your time is being wasted or that you are being mistreated? You are not obliged to stay in an unproductive situation, get out early and preserve your energy.

40.   **Man and the mirror**

Don't get carried away or feel obliged to go the extra mile by doing too much too soon. Apply balance and don't cater to him if he isn't dedicated to you. Even then, pace yourself and reflect his efforts.

41.   No disrespect or abuse

*Don't allow any room for misbehaviour of any sort.
Nip any disrespect or abuse in the bud immediately.
This could be the tip of the iceberg and be a set up
for worse to come. This person isn't ready for a
healthy relationship.*

42.   Be true to you

*Don't put on an act. Be who you are confidently
with all the quirks you may possess. Remember,
you want someone to be attracted to you genuinely,
not who you are pretending to be. This only does a
disservice to you and the dating process.*

43.   Don't force feed, plant the seed

*Ask questions about your area of interest. Is he
able to speak on it or is he clueless? Above all, is he
interested or willing to learn?*

44.   Observe his diet

*Does he have habits or behaviours that you don't
agree with; does he drink, gamble or smoke? Is
he a man of conviction for what he believes, faith
or otherwise? Is this in line with your values and
standards for a partner?*

45.   Stand proud

Would you be happy to go out in public and tell the world that this is your date if asked? If not and you would rather hide away, analyse your reasons why. Perhaps your intuition is trying to tell you something!

46.   Don't be a sweeper

If you notice something that you are not happy with, bring it up, don't sweep it under the rug and ignore it. It will only fester and cause more problems down the line.

47.   Keep your virtue

Never give your virtue to secure commitment. A man will commit on his own terms not by any coercion so don't use your body as bait.

48.   Where's the map?

Where are you going, what is your destination; being exclusive, to be married or to exist in a long-term relationship? If the end goals don't align what will you do about it. Will you settle or will you move on?

49. **Spend time in the passenger seat**

Allow him to drive the conversation, observe what topics he brings up. Be mindful that you can still see where you're going as a passenger and if you don't like the direction you can get out!

50. **Stimulate each other**

Can you have a healthy conversation that goes deeper than the surface? Do your conversations provoke thought or just provoke you? Are you happy to sign up for this?

51. **Service station**

Make sure your needs are being met, if you need consistent conversation and frequent outings, make this clear. This is the benchmark you create, if he is not able or interested to maintain this, maybe he isn't the one.

52. **Ready for the right one**

If he goes back and forth as to whether he wants to be in a relationship with you, he doesn't. Don't waste any more of your time, move on. People are usually always ready for the right person.

53. Everyone has a past

*Don't be too quick to judge, everyone has their story.
Does their story contain any unresolved pain? Do
they have a conviction? Have they worked through
their issues and turned their life around for the
better? Is this something that you can accept?*

54. Be fearless

*Be free to ask the questions that you need to. If you
don't feel able to speak freely and express yourself or
if you feel fearful, it's likely a sign telling you this isn't
a safe space.*

55. What are your terms of reference?

*Have you set your rules and regulations for the
dating process? What falls inside and outside of
scope? How often will you refer to this during the
dating process? How much tolerance will be given if
any? Don't take the chance; know your standards in
advance – then maintain them!*

56. Mind your tongue

*Don't say things just to try and make an impression.
Be your true self, authentically. This doesn't mean
that you speak everything that you are thinking. Not
everything needs a verbal response as silence can be
golden.*

57. Actions versus argument

Discern whether he is a good person through his actions. Words may not always speak the truth, but false actions are harder to disguise for a considerable time.

58. Does he align with your future family?

Speak about your future, would you like to be married and have a family together or at all. If you don't agree on this passionately, it's likely that you shouldn't be dating!

59. Believe what he shows you

He may tell you that he is single but if he keeps pulling an unexplained disappearing act then all may not be as it seems. Is he hiding something, someone or is he just not interested in you?

60. Change can be ok

Has he sparked a genuine interest in areas you need to change or grow? Was it something you were already thinking about, has this given you the impetus to change? Is he stretching you in a positive way?

61.   Accept no excuses

Don't get into the habit of accepting excuses for things not happening when they were agreed to. On the odd occasion, a reason can be offered and accepted; however, a habit shows lack of respect and lack of interest. In short, you are likely wasting your time, move on.

62.   No such thing as sexual healing whilst dating

Don't give into peer pressure or do anything against your wishes or that will make you feel uncomfortable. Whilst there is no commitment, there's no need to participate in anything sexual. This is a serious process. You don't need anything to cloud your judgement.

63.   Return to sender

You are not obliged to keep hold of anything or anyone that is not serving you. Remember, this is an audition and they are trying to secure the job. Not all applications end in success. It's like business, so don't be afraid to return your date back to their sender if their business doesn't align with yours.

64.   The booby prize

Don't play games to try and 'win'. When it comes to dating the focus is the journey as dating will have an expiry date. If you don't pay attention to the journey, you'll end up with the booby prize and think you've won when you've really lost.

65.   Protect yourself

Don't date in secrecy, be sensible, be strategic and don't put yourself in a vulnerable position. Tell friends or family where you are going and who you are with; above all, be safe.

66.   Reflect on progress

Take time by yourself to reflect on this process. Are things consistent? Are you making progress? Is it working for you? Do you feel comfortable? Ask yourself the questions you want the answers to.

67.   Are you compatible?

Don't be clouded by chemistry as it can usually always be built. Discern whether you are truly compatible with each other by how close your standards, vision and goals align.

68.   Play your cards right

Keep your cards close to your chest. Don't show him your hand to use against you and serve his own ends by lulling you into a false sense of security, where you may drop your guard. As you build trust, you can lower your guard but remember to take your time so not to leave yourself overexposed.

69. **Speak your truth**

Don't say things to go with the flow. Speak your truth even if it is in disagreement. Most of the time it is not what you say but how you say it. Don't conform to someone else's standards to fit in. If you don't feel at ease to speak up, perhaps you shouldn't be dating him.

70. **Don't take it personal**

Dating is a process, not everyone is for you so don't take it to heart if things fall apart. This departure makes the space to receive what is best for you. Don't think you've lost when you've really won!

71. **How does he handle his emotions?**

Is he quick to anger and does he have a temper? How does this make you feel? Are you worried, unbothered or scared? Does he have emotional intelligence to manage his feelings and tackle challenges in a composed way?

72. **Don't waste your own time**

Don't create a fantasy that doesn't exist; assess what is happening in real time with actual examples presented and respond accordingly. Don't repeatedly give undue time or attention to situations that do not warrant your efforts.

73.   **Stand your ground**

*Make sure you know who you are and that you
are convicted in your values, standards and way of
living. Champion who you are, don't be a pushover
and allow anyone to inveigle your principles for
their own ends.*

74.   **Value added**

*What value does he bring, what is his offering
and what does he bring to the table? Is he a goal
digger or a gold digger? Does he have his own
table or an array of skills to strengthen your table
or merely an appetite to devour?*

75.   **Acceptance**

*Accept him for who he is and what he shows you,
don't try to change him. Accept if he is a good fit
for you, and more importantly accept if he isn't a
good fit for you. Don't try to force it, just move on.*

76.   **Snap the string**

*Don't let a man keep you hanging on by a string.
Often men aren't straight forward when they're not
interested but will happily take from you and allow
you to waste your time with them, hanging on to a
lot of nothingness.*

77. **More than skin deep**

Look beneath the surface and don't get caught up on the things that are presented at a superficial level such as looks, labels, cars, status and such, as this is likely lust. Real attraction shouldn't be based upon skin deep preferences but focus on a man's character and who he is at his core.

78. **A game of chances**

You can perhaps try again if you don't succeed at first if the reasons were not toxic. However, don't get caught up in a cycle with the same person as it can breed toxicity. How many chances will you permit before you call time on the relationship?

Part Four

The Meal Plan

Now you're a team, the hard work has just begun and so has the fun! Maintaining a healthy relationship is a daily decision both parties willingly take, just like eating. We need to eat to sustain life but what is on your menu?

Picture a delicious healthy meal full of vitamins and nutrients, natural foods featuring all the colours of the rainbow. Imagine the beneficial qualities this has for the body. A healthy relationship is like good food, nourishing, energising and full of goodness. It benefits the mind, body and soul. However, it's not as simple as just eating good food; you need to invest in it, put in the work to learn which qualities are present in which ingredients. Being mindful about what produce is in season, how to prepare it to maintain its minerals and most importantly how to harvest and preserve it to sustain longevity so that you can reap what you sow.

Now, imagine a plate full of junk food products, you may enjoy the taste; but what affects will this have? It may be challenging to maintain a good diet with all the distractions of unhealthy offerings, but we all know what is best for us. Living on a diet of poor food choices will likely create toxins within the body resulting in poor health and impacting on how effectively we can undertake our daily activities. This may not be noticeable at a glance but will gradually creep up on you and snatch your quality of life.

This can be applied to relationships; are we taking the time to carefully prepare what we consume each day? Are we cultivating to include a variety of the goodness we need, or are we rushing meals just so we can say that we have eaten? In a healthy relationship we want to feel energised through the abundance of positive exchange. Temptations may always be present but if we want to enjoy relationships at their best, we need to take the actions necessary to keep it fresh or even to make it spicy; either way we want to maintain its health and not allow it to decay.

These reminders encourage you to be intentional about how you are feeding your relationship. Is it thriving on a healthy dose of communication and accountability or are you surviving on a junk food diet of arguments and neglect? Do you feel sustained or do you feel sick? Is it time for a detox?

Reminders 79 to 101 - *A Happy Healthy Relationship*

79.   Hold each other accountable

Speak up and don't let things that you are unhappy or uncomfortable with slide by; seek a resolution early.

80.   Build and inspire

Work together and better each other, encourage one another to do great things. Make plans together and discuss your vision for the future.

81.   Consistent servicing

Be mindful that you are looking out for each other and supporting each other's wellbeing - mind, body and spirit. Don't take your partner for granted and begin to let things slip. Keep managing and meeting each other's expectations.

82.   **Meet challenges head on**

Do not evade situations in hope that they will disappear or resolve themselves. Confrontation is better than retreat in this instance as dealing with challenges avoids them being repeated.

83.   **Learn forgiveness**

Don't hold a grudge, learn to forgive and let things go. Grudges only build up toxins in your relationship and hold you both as hostages.

84.   **Mind sex**

The brain is the most powerful organ in the human body. Maintain intimacy by working to stimulate each other's minds constantly.

85.   **Willing to leave**

Don't put up with repeated disrespect or abuse for the sake of a relationship. Know your worth, always remember it and be prepared to act on it.

86.   **Greener grass**

All grass needs tending to if it is to thrive; it remains healthy and vibrant where it is looked after. Keep yours well-manicured to avoid it becoming overgrown and full of weeds.

87.   **Respect each other**

Work together, everything doesn't need to be a battle and it is ok to have a moment for you. Avoid battling each other and battle oppositions together.

88.   **Make your own traditions**

Learn what works well for your relationship and establish new ways of doing things.

89.   **Keep on dating**

You've come this far, don't lose the chemistry that keeps you connected. Taking compatibility for granted will encourage things to become stagnant.

90.   **Surprise, surprise!**

Don't be too predictable and allow things to become stale. Continue to learn from each other and stimulate the mind in new ways.

91.   **Be transparent**

Remember you are a team so be honest, be open and be willing to share with each other.

92.   Happy surroundings

Not everyone is for you, be mindful of intruders and don't let people who are not for you inveigle your union.   Be mindful of some friends or family and don't take advice from bitter people.

93.   Let him be a man

Men are not women; they can process things differently and may take an interest in things you have limited capacity for. Remember you're a team so be encouraging and give him space for him to be.

94.   Space to be a woman

Women are not men; we can process things differently and may take an interest in things men have limited capacity for. Although you're a team, be encouraged and take space to be.

95.   Seek wise counsel

It's ok to ask for advice from someone you both appreciate and respect. Sometimes it may be necessary, especially at pivotal points in your relationship.

96.   **No to abuse**

Don't tolerate any sort of abuse in any way shape or form. Don't ignore its existence, no matter how slight, as it can undermine you and creep up to devour you completely. Get help or get out.

97.   **Mind your business**

Your relationship is your business; it's your business to make it work every day. It takes a continual effort to achieve success. Take care of it and it will in turn take care of you.

98.   **Practice makes practice**

There's always room for improvement so keep on at it and don't get complacent. Practice doesn't make perfect as things change as the earth revolves, so they'll always be new things to consider. If we think things are perfect, then we may stop trying so keep on practicing to keep on improving and growing with each other.

99.   **Can't undo what has been done**

Words and actions can be weapons, choose them wisely and be careful how you choose to communicate with your partner.

100. Lead and receive

Play your positions and lead in your areas of strength, teach each other and maintain balance to avoid one person taking on an entire load: be a help not a hindrance.

101. Focus on the marriage not the wedding

Many marriages fail, weddings rarely do; don't confuse the two!

Conclusion

When All is Said and Done

We all have an opinion about what makes for a successful relationship and no two relationships are the same. What is the culture you want to create in your relationship? We often pay too much attention to what is happening all around us to create an ideal of how we should be experiencing relationships. Artificial perspectives can create a stronghold within us that takes hard work and perseverance to remove.

These reminders can help by motivating us to manage our own expectations through creating our specific boundaries and principles in relationships. They can serve to encourage us to better understand who we are by how we communicate with ourselves and with others. They can inspire us to seek within and pay close attention to our intuition and to be alert for what provokes or triggers us. They should be a reference point for how we conduct ourselves and what we accept if we want to be successful when it comes to healthy relationships.

Like the freedom of the first breath we took when we were born it should feel like a natural process. We shouldn't allow relationships to stifle our breathing or asphyxiate us. They should be a breath of fresh air and breathe life into our existence encouraging us to prosper. They should challenge us in a healthy way that inspires us to grow far away from toxic or polluting fumes. Agree, disagree, question or challenge, hopefully you've found something valuable within these reminders that can be a kiss of life to your current or future relationship.

The Relationship ABCs

. . .

I created the *Relationship ABCs* as a useful tool to help individuals begin to form healthy relationships with themselves and beyond. It provides three key reference categories, from which many things can be aligned. These categories can help you to consider where you are and more significantly where you need to grow.

To begin to have healthy relationships, we each need to have an awareness of and work on our *Relationship ABCs*; continually. This should be a never-ending process, as we are evolving beings there is always room for improvement. Even maintenance takes consistent work!

Your *Relationship ABCs* are reflected in your approach and are cemented in how you treat, value, and honour yourself. It is a demonstration of self-love. We all have things we can work on to improve our relationships, what are you doing to enhance yours?

Relationship ABCs

Attitude	*What is your outlook and perspective; what are your dreams and goals, are you working towards them?*
Behaviour	*What does your lifestyle say about you, do you act with integrity? What are your habits and how do you treat yourself mentally, physically, spiritually, emotionally, financially, and socially?*
Character	*What is your foundation; what are your core values and principles; what guides, centres and balances you?*

Source: *TrueRelations.UK*

For tips, tools and testimony, visit the True Relations Platform online at **TrueRelations.UK**.

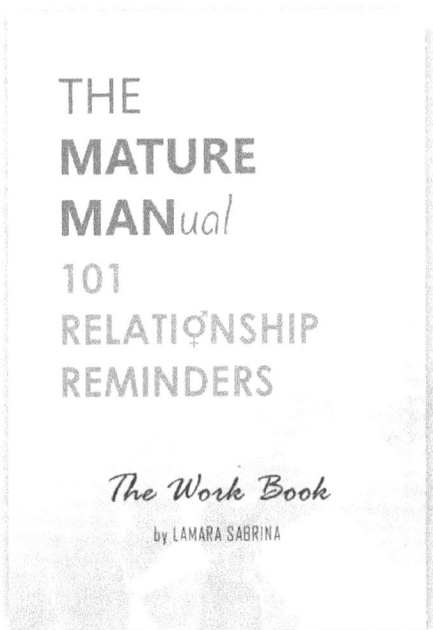

THE
MATURE
MANual
101
RELATIONSHIP
REMINDERS

The Work Book
by LAMARA SABRINA

The workbook to support this book
is available online exclusively at:
TrueRelations.UK

Other books in this series are available online:

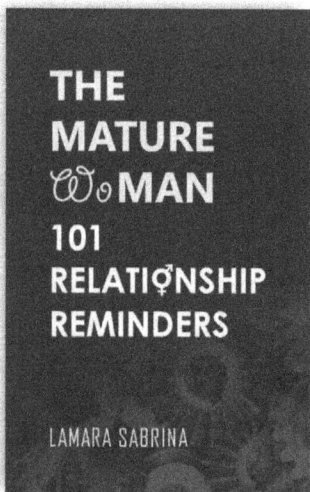

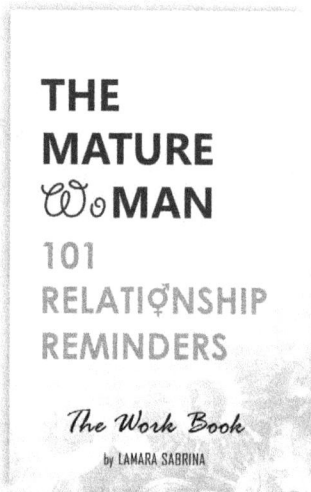

THE
MATURE
Wo MAN
101
RELATIONSHIP
REMINDERS

LAMARA SABRINA

THE
MATURE
Wo MAN
101
RELATIONSHIP
REMINDERS

The Work Book

by LAMARA SABRINA

Acknowledgements

. . .

Firstly, and fundamentally, I give thanks to the creator and to the heirs beneath my wings - One Love Always! Much respect to the friends and family who held me up by listening and providing feedback to my many ideas.

Give thanks to those who encouraged or inspired this book either directly or indirectly. Much appreciation to my editor Karma and to Donna and Matthew who reviewed and commented on this book before it was published

A special thank you to Amanda and Keith for writing the foreword; your words encourage me to continue my work in serving others and further enthusiasm to proceed.

Finally, and fondly, thank you to all the booklovers for reading this book; I hope it remains of great value.

About the Author

. . .

Founder of True Relations UK, an online coaching service, Lamara uses her personal testimony along with her education and experiences to work with people across the world. An experienced communication strategist and mentor, she took the decision to step away from her corporate career and fulfil her passion to help people in a more personal way.

She envisages this manual will serve as a tool, for all women young and old, to open conversations about healthy relationships. As it is when we gain the knowledge that we can begin to form an understanding to make the necessary applications needed for success.

....
....
....
....
....
....
....
....
....
....
....
....
....
....
....
....
....
....
....
....

....

....

....

....

....

....

....

....

....

....

....

....

....

....

....

....

....

....

....

....
....
....
....
....
....
....
....
....
....
....
....
....
....
....
....
....
....
....
....

SPREAD THE WORD

#TheMatureManual
#TheMatureMan
#101RelationshipReminders
#TheMatureWoman
#TrueRelationsUK
#LamaraSabrina

Give Thanks

www.ingramcontent.com/pod-product-compliance
Lightning Source LLC
Chambersburg PA
CBHW060640280326
41933CB00012B/2096